ON THE WATER

Wakeboarding

by Rachel Grack

BLASTOFF! READERS 2

BLASTOFF! READERS, AN IMPRINT OF BELLWETHER MEDIA BY FLUTTERBEE

Blastoff! Readers are carefully developed by literacy experts to build reading stamina and move students toward fluency by combining standards-based content with developmentally appropriate text.

Level 1 provides the most support through repetition of high-frequency words, light text, predictable sentence patterns, and strong visual support.

Level 2 offers early readers a bit more challenge through varied sentences, increased text load, and text-supportive special features.

Level 3 advances early-fluent readers toward fluency through increased text load, less reliance on photos, advancing concepts, longer sentences, and more complex special features.

★ Blastoff! Universe

This edition first published in 2027 by Bellwether Media, Inc.

For information regarding permission, write to Bellwether Media, Inc., Attention: Permissions Department, 3500 American Blvd W, Suite 150, Bloomington, MN 55431.

Library of Congress Cataloging-in-Publication Data is available at www.loc.gov or upon request from the publisher.

ISBN: 9798898800611 (hardcover)
ISBN: 9798898801854 (ebook)

Editor: Kieran Downs Series Designer: Josh Brink Designer: Laura Sowers

Printed in the United States of America, North Mankato, MN.

Table of Contents

Ride the Wake

Wakeboarding is a popular water sport. People stand on a special board as they are pulled behind a motorboat.

People wakeboard on lakes, rivers, and oceans.

Top Place to Wakeboard

Lake Powell, Utah and Arizona, United States

There are many kinds of wakeboards. The length is based on the rider's weight. Different **rockers** help with turning.

Boots and **bindings** hold the rider's feet to the board.

Wakeboarders often ride behind boats. They hold onto ropes.

At **cable parks**, people can wakeboard without a boat. Cables pull wakeboarders along tracks.

cable park

Wakeboarders wear life jackets. **Impact vests** and helmets keep wakeboarders safe during **wipeouts**.

Different ropes and handles work better for different wakeboard rides.

What Wakeboarders Need

Getting Started on Wakeboarding

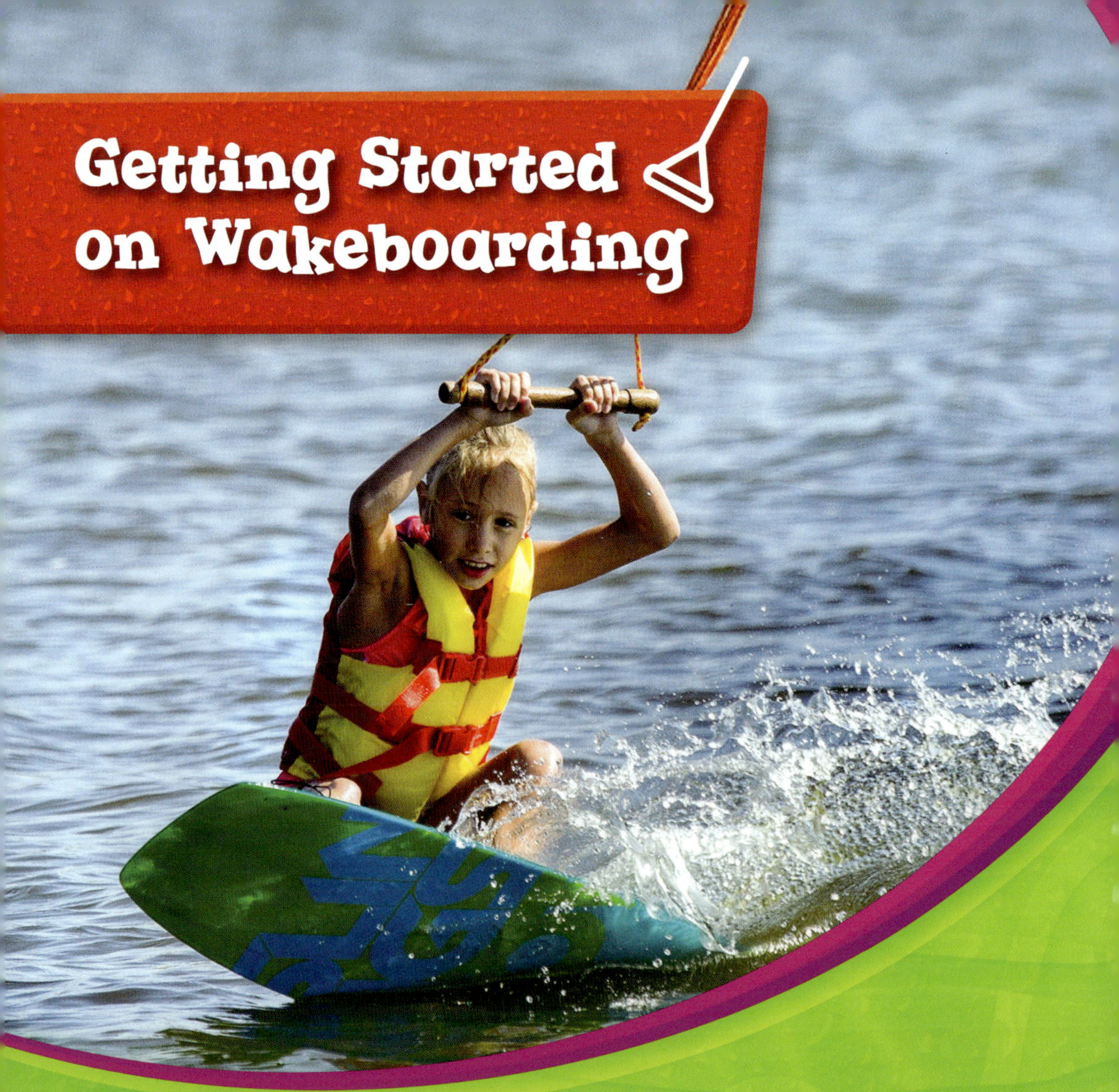

Beginning wakeboarders often start out on larger boards. Long boards with smooth rockers make it easier to learn.

Beginners often use short ropes.

Wakeboarders strap their feet in the boots. They sit down in the water while holding the handle.

They pull their knees
toward their chests.

Wakeboarders stay seated with their arms stretched out as the boat starts to move.

As the boat goes faster, the board rises. Wakeboarders slowly stand up.

Wakeboarders turn behind the boat. They zip back and forth.

Wakeboarding Tricks

ollie

surface 360

tailgrab

boardslide

They jump off of the **wake**. Some wakeboarders do tricks and spins.

Go Wakeboarding!

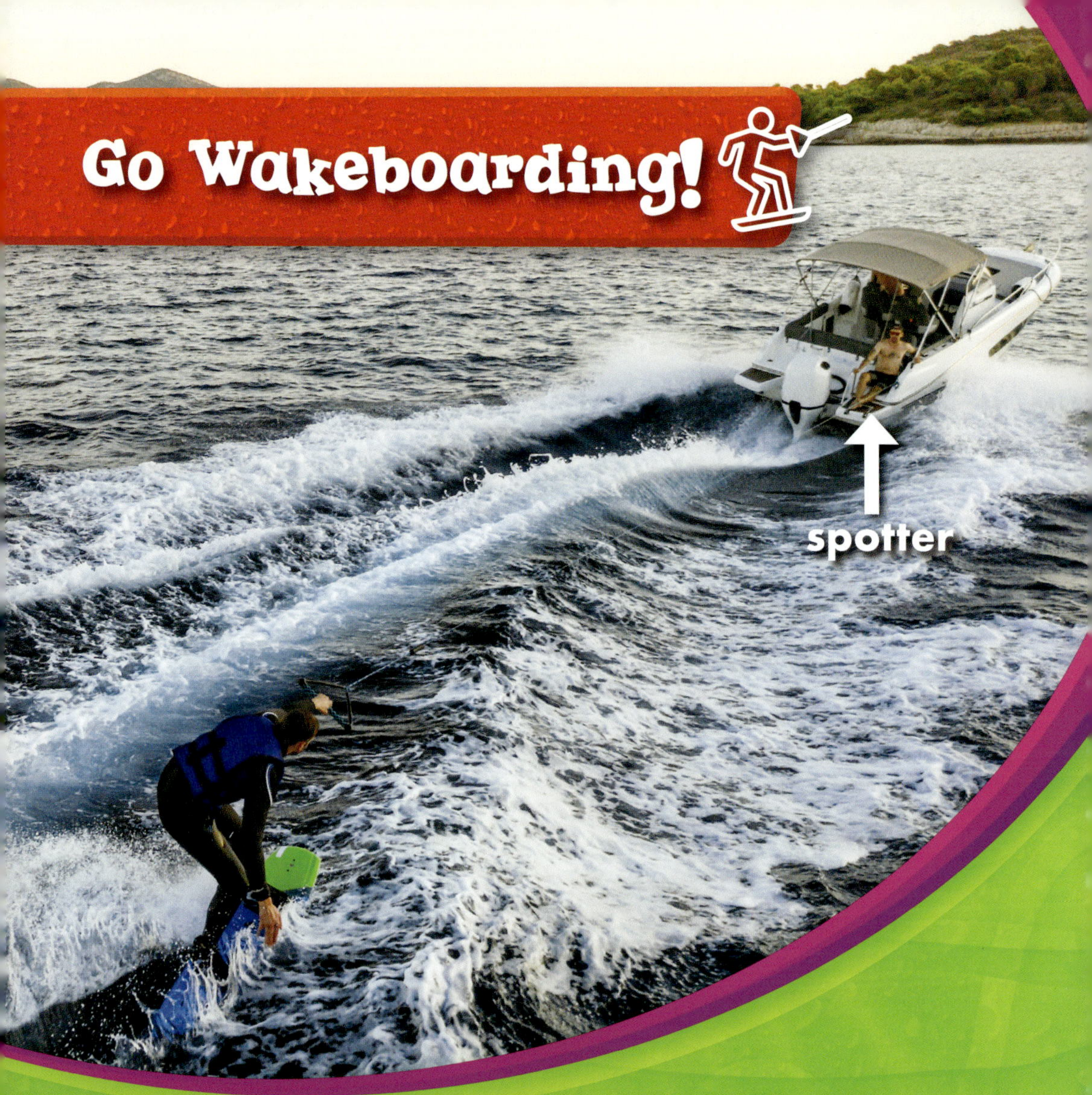

Wakeboarders wear safety gear. They always have a **spotter**.

They should only ride during the day. Time for fun on the water!

Glossary

bindings—parts that connect a wakeboarder's feet to the board

cable parks—water sport parks where wakeboarders are pulled by a cable system instead of a boat

impact vests—life jackets with padding that protect wakeboarders from hard falls

rockers—the curves of a wakeboard

spotter—a person in a boat who watches wakeboarders in case of a fall

wake—the track of waves behind a motorboat

wipeouts—falls

To Learn More

AT THE LIBRARY

Catena, Melissa. *Water Safety.* Minneapolis, Minn.: Jump!, 2025.

Grack, Rachel. *Kitesurfing.* Minneapolis, Minn.: Bellwether Media, 2027.

Grack, Rachel. *Water Skiing.* Minneapolis, Minn.: Bellwether Media, 2027.

ON THE WEB

FACTSURFER

Factsurfer.com gives you a safe, fun way to find more information.

1. Go to www.factsurfer.com.
2. Enter "wakeboarding" into the search box and click .
3. Select your book cover to see a list of related content.

Index

The images in this book are reproduced through the courtesy of: New Africa, front cover (top), pp. 11, 19 (surface 360); Delmas Lehman, front cover (bottom); WoodHunt, p. 3; master1305, p. 4; mseidelch, pp. 4-5; Juan Carlos Munoz, p. 5; KopoPhoto, pp. 6-7; 2tun, p. 7; Maksym Fesenko, p. 8; Aerial Film Studio, pp. 8-9; nms1980, p. 10; Anatolii kostyk, pp. 10-11; A_Lesik, pp. 12-13; Roman babakin, p. 13; Cavan-Images, p. 14; Gerain0812, pp. 14-15; fesenko, p. 16; Olya Komarova, pp. 16-17; Anna Moskvina, pp. 18-19; Yobro10, p. 19 (ollie); Mickes Photos, p. 19 (tailgrab); andrijapajic, p. 19 (broadslide); Lukas Gojda, pp. 20-21; Jatupon, p. 21; Petro, p. 23.